TED McNULTY

ON THE BLOCK

SALMON POETRY

Published in 1995 by
Salmon Publishing Ltd,
Upper Fairhill, Galway

© Ted McNulty 1995

The moral right of the author has been asserted

The Publishers gratefully acknowledge the support of The Arts Council

A catalogue record for this book is available from the British Library

ISBN 1 897648 20 0

Cover etching Peter Hogan
Cover design by Poolbeg Group Services Ltd
Set by Poolbeg Group Services Ltd in Goudy 11.5/14
Printed by Colour Books, Baldoyle Industrial Estate, Dublin 13

To Sheila
and Aisling, Conor, Niav

ACKNOWLEDGEMENTS

The author is grateful to the editors of the following publications in which some of these poems first appeared:

In Ireland: *Acorn*, *The Connacht Tribune*, *Drumlin*, *Extended Wings*, *Force 10*, *Honest Ulsterman*, *The Irish Times*, *Poetry Ireland Review*, *Windows Selections*, *Womanspirit*

In Britain: *European Judaism*, *Irish Studies Review*, *Iron*, *Lines Review*, *The Observer*, *Oxford Poetry*, *The Spectator*

In America: *The Hudson Review*, *Maryland Poetry Review*, *Ploughshares*, *Southern Poetry Review*

The author also acknowledges the support of the Arts Council through the Arts Council-Aer Lingus Travel Awards programme.

CONTENTS

PART I – NEW YORK

The Tenor – 1941   3
Moscowitz – 1944   4
Frankie – 1944   5
St Joe's – 1946   6
'The Third Man' – 1949   7
Commuter – 1958   8
The End of Them   10
Soldier Boy   11
Labor Day   12

PART II – THE CRYSTAL BALLROOM

The Red Nail   15
The Crystal Ballroom   16
The Medicine   17
Doc   18
Reading Solzhenitsyn   19
Rosa Bonheur's 'The Horse Fair'   20
Lilac   21
New Man   22
The Girl on the Northern Line   23
The Model Plane   24
Catch   25
Close   26
White   27
Another Country   28

PART III – TAHITI

Landing   31
Slats   32
Ma Ma   33
Bone   34

Cookfires   35
,   36
Mail Plane   37
The Angel of Romance   38
The Edge   39
Legionnaire   40
The Wave   41

PART IV – IMMIGRANT

The Immigrant   45
Straw and Whins   46
The Hurley   47
Gallagan's Hill   48
The Horse Fair   49
Pair of Shoes   50
Cattleboat   51
Kind of a Man   52
Cemetery, Glencree   53
Coal   54

PART V – AROUND ST STEPHEN'S GREEN

McGwinn and Son – Wexford St   57
The Brick – Chatham St   58
Dublin Flat   59
Grogan's – South William St   60
Basement – By Stephen's Green   61
Plastic Bag – Stephen's Green   62
St Teresa's – Clarendon St   63
Touching Mercury – Kildare St   64
The Cave – Stephen's Green   65
A Small Cafe – Montague St   66
The Playwright – Harcourt St   67
Scratch Cards – Cuffe St   68

PART I

NEW YORK

THE TENOR – NEW YORK 1941

That night rain put a shine
on New York as we passed under
a filigree glass marquee,
doormen bowing to our tickets,
my mother and father so proud
to show me one of their own
singing the melodies of Moore,
the great tenor, hair shining,
his tuxedo with the green sash
in the gold of Carnegie Hall,
a place good enough for Rockefeller
my father nudged me to remember
and now I see his eyes full
as if suddenly he was a millionaire
who had come from the land
where the road to Ballyduff
was made of marble
and a Count sang in the square.

MOSCOWITZ – NEW YORK 1944

I spent the war in Moscowitz's
candy-brown store full of boys
drinking cola, orange soda
from bottles iced in a tin tub
while overhead Spitfires, B-17s
dangled above Old Moscowitz
along his counters of caramels,
pretzels, ghost masks, watching me
take up a seat without spending.
And the day I stared back in a way
that called him a name to his face
over tall stacks of evening papers
he touched me still with change,
selling me sweets skin of the fingers
inky with news from the Eastern Front.

FRANKIE – NEW YORK 1944

Italian kid with hair
on his fingers, Frankie,
king of the block,
says he'll go first, watches
from a hill in the park
a traffic light turn green,
the bus go into gear –
then his shoes slushing
past the line of us.
American Flyer sleigh at his side
he hunches on the run,
falls on the pine slats,
a belly-flop slapping metal
red runners on packed snow
as he blades into white sky
a long swoop down the hill,
over sidewalk and kerb
across the icy street,
passing in front of the bus
by this much,
and that's what it took
to be king in New York.

ST JOE'S – NEW YORK 1946

The young nun's only victory
over the boys in the back row –
I always raised my hand,
asked for help with maths

and she would lean over me,
give me the smell of her soap,
touch my copybook with her hand,
her finger on my sum

as I bent close to her skin
pretending weak eyes,
the big lunk of me,
new hair growing every day.

It happened during history –
a wish with a will of its own
fought its way out and slyly
I said the word

that brought her down the aisle,
eyes blue as gas on a burner,
and my cheeks already blushing
I waited for her hand.

'THE THIRD MAN' – NEW YORK 1949

My friend the rain
making water stars
in streams of light
down streets of cinemas
that never closed.

Duffled schoolboy
on the shine
of Times Square
into a morning movie
full of damp men
and with the touch
on my leg
I had to decide.

On the screen Vienna
after the war,
in shadows Harry Lime
selling black market
penicillin but his girl
still loves him.

And I'm thinking
no matter what I've done
there could be a girl
who'd want me
for no good reason.

Home on a city bus
the windows steamed,
and with the finger
I rubbed the glass
looking out for her.

COMMUTER – NEW YORK 1958

Came the day
I knew I had gone
too far in America,
away from the Bronx
and the parish,
in with white faces
who lived here-and-now
with no before, no stories
of fields of potatoes
turning into stones,
my sense of that
sure as the red
on my father's face
rawed on drumlins
and so deep it spread
onto mine.

That morning the touch
of our suits
on an underground train
sparking downtown
to Madison Avenue station,
but I don't get off
with them, keep going
down the tunnel
into the before, stand
among murmurs of men
in Cavan grey

until dreams snap
in the blue electric flash
of circuit breakers
at the last stop,
and I'm here at the end
of New York City
with a briefcase
full of earth.

THE END OF THEM

Over there I know you
in the brown suit coat
with the blue trousers
shiny on folding chairs
of funeral parlours tonight
up and down the Bronx,
your hair wet, parted,
Sunday white shirt
for the wakes
of park bench friends
come over with you
from Cavan to find
their city in the glass,
and you would be wondering
which sons and daughters
will come in the door
before Father Hugh begins
to say the words
that can't be true –
as it was in the beginning
so it shall be in the end.

SOLDIER BOY

Up river from New York
the reserve fleet
of rusty troopships
left over from the war
wallow on the Hudson,
send me signals
in the clitter of riggings
above the steel hulls
of lost battalions –
as time runs back
to when the clocker
called the time for war
and I played toy soldiers
on the carpet of a room,
put down the enemy
with flicks of fingers,
advanced with infantry
who once packed the ships
still here to carry me away.

LABOR DAY

His flower in a coffee can
beside loose bricks
ledged on a city rowhouse
gerrymandered for six kids,
roosts of rooms, tilting floors,
swayback roof sloping
toward a Brooklyn shipyard
still as a world war watch.

Pat Mahoney, old boilermaker,
the belly on him,
down to two cigars a day,
living off the mailman's pouch
and luncheonette shank stew,
fries sunken in the gravy,
but hungry for the past,

leans into the morning
from the brown of a room,
tips a jug over the flower,
pouring as if it was milk
into six kitchen mugs,
then hangs his stars and stripes,
held to the ledge with bricks
from the shipyard.

PART II

THE CRYSTAL BALLROOM

THE RED NAIL

Inside my mother's sandal
dark smooth from the sweat,
the press of her body
into hollows of the heel.
Straps fingery white
around where a toenail
coloured strawberry
came out for all to see
something that was beyond me.

THE CRYSTAL BALLROOM

Back of the bar
a mirror searches
for the face
to go with the song
his mother sang
of a pale moon rising
above the mountain.

He follows the song
to a white pavilion
its ballroom turning
in the crystal of a glass,
and shoulders
through the dancers,
mother drunk.

THE MEDICINE

On waiting room benches
of clinics for children
he sat in a daydream gown
slipped on when he blinked
at the globes of the lights,
and having found the way
to take himself anywhere
he kept it like medicine
that made everything yesterday,
himself someone else
yet close like a cousin
in a life of nothing wrong,
and now back on a clinic
bench worn by the sliding
he blinks, and looks easy.

DOC

Alone with him,
the shush of us through leaves
and I don't know where I'm going.

No words of consultation,
more the thought
of only the wind between
that closeness with a man

who leads me across walled grounds
to stand beside a pond
that receives me in its eye,
gives me back myself

and I fear lest I waver
as autumn tosses the day,
but the pond holds me still

in a time when I lived
in a house of a thousand windows,
the memory diamond-wired

of two men among fallen colours
sensing the place to stop
and nothing need be said.

READING SOLZHENITSYN

The prison ark
in the paper-white field
near the Arctic Circle

a long barrack
built of words,
carrying its men

free from hope
into the scape
of a tundra moon.

They are wrapped
in blankets of each other,
only beards between them

soft as glaze
on the eye of an exile
longing for a voyage

in an ark of men,
flames from its prow
burning a passage.

ROSA BONHEUR'S 'THE HORSE FAIR'
Oil on Canvas (1853)

So as not to be bothered
she dressed as a man
at the horse fair,
painting in her head
the curves of haunch,
arch of rib, fetlock,
eyes of horses like fires
in barny light.

Now that day has dried
and for so long I stand
before the painting
I feel inside her ghost,
her eyes under mine,
blending us like roan, brindle
as we linger in a gallery
looking like a man alone.

LILAC

The wood smelling
of its paint,
so alive the heat
falling from an August
when I trimmed bushes
beside our house.
Sweat in the eyes
as a blind rush
of something in me
flashed the shears
at what was growing,
the branch that rose
to our bedroom window
down in a slash.
It was years
before it came to me,
the cutting of her lilac
was the start.

NEW MAN

When my head
fell from the bed
make the best of it
I said, listen
to the floor

and I heard
the rumble of the mill
still in the wood,
rasp, split, sighs
of timbers

dreamed I rolled
in white pine shavings,
sap, cedar chips
until all covered over
I felt new

and back in bed
full of knowing how
to keep myself together,
not caring when she says
I am a wooden man.

THE GIRL ON THE NORTHERN LINE

'I'm not myself' she says
and anger streams
into her hair
until it grows long
as the threads unravelling
in closets of the marriage.

I see her draw the strands
into the roots of her head,
then waver through crowds
on falling stairs to platforms
of the Northern Line,

where swirls of wind unfurl
her hair on airstreams
down the tunnel to Waterloo
and its black strings curl
the waiting shoes,

then sweep the rails for power
as if to turn great pulley wheels
winding back the strands
of people twisting in her hair
beside me as I sleep.

THE MODEL PLANE

Shaving the wood
and smelling the glue
I shaped a model plane
that would hang over me
strung from the ceiling,
grow up with me, full-size,
and in the cockpit
I'd race the propellers,
cross lines and coasts
of charts that took me
all my years to states
of mind where no one
ever had a name,
faces patches of colour
like maps on the wall
of a new child's room
where I play with my son
while above a fuselage sways.

CATCH

His fastball a line
white across the lawn
trailing its colour
into my glove,
the power of my son
bursting into the palm.
My hand on fire
I take time, turn
the baseball as if
I see a broken stitch,
then throw back
the pitch curving forever
across that summer
we gave each other
our best stuff.

CLOSE

First card in years
from a son in the States –
still scuba diving,
been to the islands.

From the bottom
of a cloud of Silk Cut
I see him above me
looking the years
since we touched,
brown hair, thick legs,
tank on his back
trailing white beads
through my smoke,
and I let him go by
as if close was enough.

WHITE

Someone in me says
pick up the man
and we rise together
in Tuscan forests
to the monastery,
his cassock a white
that fills the car
and he silent, hooded,
smelling of this world,
fish fry, vinegar chips
supper on his breath
turning me away
from the light of him.

ANOTHER COUNTRY

I travel with my cigarettes,
long Muratti specials,
on brown Italian trains
that leave me in cities
to get on as best I can.
Americans everywhere,
the sound of them
taking me back to a wife
who's gone, lost like a ring,
but in that street stall
was her face among the figurines.
I turn and hide away
in the summer haze
of yet another foreign city
until at dark a key,
the bag, left on the bed,
an ashtray by the window.

PART III

TAHITI

LANDING

Night plane
across the Pacific
on a web of signals,
its black windows
spotted with stars,
drops on a line
to blue runways,
touches down on scent
of orchids and rain.

*

The long Peugeot,
an ambulance
made into a taxi,
takes shortcut roads,
dips into ruts
made deep over years,
trounce of the past
tossing my head.

SLATS

On the edge, a coastal man,
I write myself a new home
with gatherings from islands,
pile them over the past
then lay meanings that roof,
beam, half cover me with sticks
so my lines are sun and dark
slats across my eyes.

MA MA

Ankle deep across the reef
I gather octopus for bait
as I fish with Ma Ma
in an open boat,
a white man alone
with an old ocean woman,

while Mickey Mouse plays
on the face of her watch,
hiding then showing up
like magic with each turn
of her wrist as she jigs
the lines.

All morning the slide,
suck of the hull
as sun turns my colour
until I see myself
the fool to have come
to this last resort,
but then beside me
the girl from the dream,
taking me under the green
of her old umbrella.

BONE

An infant choking on a bone
from the fish that I caught,

feed bread, finger wet pink
glisten, remedies half-heard

in the race of storm
past the hut by the sea

pound of breakers
punching concussion in the air

great falls of wave
dancing the table, trembling her

until the child swallows
then coughs up

a curl of silver bone
in the bubbles on her tongue.

COOKFIRES

An orange evening
on the rim of a lagoon
full of the ticking
of hollow wooden drums
and along the shore
cookfires make caves of light
as circles of families close
in rings on New Year's Eve.
I draw my mind
into a circle of its own,
set the parts talking
until they leave me
to drift on smoke
from roast pork and yams.

,

I try to tap
into the past
for I've forgotten
the face
that goes
with this feeling

my hands waiting
over the portable
until a finger
drops on a key
and commas rise
row upon row
they field the page

under the oil lamp
their black turning gold
like hair in waves
on utter white

bring back
that morning
at the kitchen table
when she smiled
and looking up
took me through the ceiling.

MAIL PLANE

Her letters
have stopped
but the habit
of having them
follows me
to this dot
on a map
and the strip
where a plane
with the mail
comes to land,
the pouch
her red gold
like a fire
on the sand.

THE ANGEL OF ROMANCE

The spread of my hand
like cane slats
on the back of a chair
waits for the lean

wet heat of her skin
through the blouse,
shoulder blades
impressing my fingers

and the palm tells a fortune
of the heaviness of angels.

THE EDGE

Thistling palm spears
and smack of leaves
big as elephant ears,

but her husband
crashing through the rain
is what I listen for

as she holds me down
on the mat of her hut –
the kerosene lamp
swaying above us.

He won't come home,
she says, too drunk,
far away, other island,
working cane fields.

I am offering myself
to her gods
as if I were someone else

for I see his machete
standing in the corner
its edge a line in the dark

and my head rolls back
to a time of tended lawns,
trim hedge, bed of flowers,
a house I once painted white.

LEGIONNAIRE

Broken men here
in red tin sheds
locked barracks
behind the wire.

I feel what happens
with a feral sense
that sees

the legionnaire nod
as if to say
he would break me

like these island men
who will not serve
the Frenchman's army

and who tried to hide
like me in shelly beds
along an archipelago
of black pearls.

THE IMMIGRANT

The Yank in me
rides the sound
of loose chippings
on a Cavan road,

a neighbour
taking me along
to the cattle auction
in a shed of wet coats

where I'm the stranger
in a ring of men
but close to the creatures,
smells old as straw.

Driving back, the radio
plays 'California Blue'
as I go in two directions,
neither of them home

While road stones crackle
the hard words of immigrants,
telling me now I must live
in the cut of myself.

STRAW AND WHINS

A low townland in Cavan
with no one left in it,
hedges narrowing lanes
down to Lough Sheelin,
and I piece myself together
with what I find in the place,
make me into a man
of straw, whins, roots,
and float along the shore,
lean toward the whispers
of the reeds telling me
look here for my faces –
father, uncles, cousins
come back from New York,
happy enough to be buried
standing up, out in the air,
under the lid of the sky.

THE HURLEY

The hurley of my father,
eighty years since it broke
the shin of a priest
playing the Sunday game
at Ballymachugh,
an aimed hit, they said,
that split the wood

and the hurley kept
in a corner of the kitchen
to mind the long time
the family's been rising
out of the white breath
of Cavan

and here I am on a Sunday
breaking the religion,
a split that's standing
in a corner like the hurley
full of a power of its own.

GALLAGAN'S HILL

They had him in this yard
but what can I see
for all the changes
of eighty years since
my grandfather was beaten
with a bundle of whins

because one of his sons
passed a test for the Royal
Irish Constabulary,
the father put on his knees
the night the men came,
known by their shoes

and the family made watch
until he gave in
swore the boy wouldn't –
the brothers all left
after that for New York,

son of the last come back.
I stand in the yard
by the cottage now
a Spar selling Maxol
where thin roads cross
the way to Ballyduff

while on Gallagan's Hill
a tractor watches,
the red of a butt up there
in the grey.

THE HORSE FAIR

Over the river into the grey
to catch rings in the air
from hammers on fiery shoes
and clatter on cobbles
wet and dungy from horses
for sale in their old coats
standing in the drizzle
of a Dublin Sunday market
where bareback a boy, his rein
a hand on the mane of a dray,
stolen, painted over with spots,
joy-rides down King Street
chasing a Volvo until hooves
kick away a tail light
and I shy of feelings
from years ago cheer in silence
the horse and the boy.

PAIR OF SHOES

He worries he's buying
his last pair of shoes
the tired man, not me,
and the last train
leaving him standing,
that's not me either,
so when I miss the 6:10
I go down on the track,
come out of Galway
running the sleepers
into a night of red dots
curving toward Athenry,
big strides and the breath
puffing me up into a giant,
I'm taller than the signals,
leap over bridges, stations,
and when a goods train
hits my shoe I brush it
into a field of brown flowers
the carpet in a parlour
where once I tripped electric
trains off their tracks,
Empire State King Kong Kid
dumb tough dreamer
in the new pair of shoes.

CATTLEBOAT

The tongue on him
from drinking out the days,
and the house crying,
he leaves for the docks
to board his ship
the cattleboat from Cork
that tips and arks
its way to Libya, the decks
iron drums the hooves
pound as they shift
in a hull rolling over
long bones of sea,
and on watch alone
his fingers touch lightly
the helm, playing away
waves to gentle
a thousand head below,
the good in him
finding its way.

KIND OF A MAN

How long will he stand
as around him a bull
circles closer
edging in all afternoon
its hooves making rings
in the field
and soft the first touch
of horn on his trouser
shivering the cloth
as it passes,
the steam of the thing
and head low it lunks
round on him again
the eye not letting go
as if the animal knows
the kind of man he is.

CEMETERY, GLENCREE

I come upon German soldiers
in greatcoats of rain
under wintergreen trees,
their graves in a Wicklow glen.

Warriors who fell from clouds,
washed in from the last war,
receive me in silence,
I am not of their kind.

Around them laurel, holly,
ribbons black, white, red
for they are kept by their own

and in the woods I hear
a boot step on a branch
as if a father was coming
through ancient trees
to look after his son.

COAL

Father on the coal docks,
I have spent my winters
in your smoking hand,
the butt turned in
to warm me in cave
and cup of the palm,
its skin cracked black
from years on the shovel.

Now as I am pulled
on chains of river lights
along the quay, I say:
Ganger, call my name,
roster me with shovellers,
remember me the fist
of tough flesh padded,
smell of tobacco, coal,
the heat once
inside a hand gone dark.

PART V

AROUND ST STEPHEN'S GREEN

MᶜGWINN AND SON – WEXFORD STREET

Too many butchers
on the street
and alone in his shop
pretending to be busy
he suddenly hears
the long curse
he never knew was in him,
the throat on its own
with a shout
that goes back to the day
he put on his father's apron
and his mouth
turned into a purse.

THE BRICK – CHATHAM STREET

Cold enough the night
he threw a brick
at the moon
as it crossed
a shop window,
then waited
for the sky to flash
blue light
and the van
to take him back.

DUBLIN FLAT

I like to hear
the vacuum going,
rushy air,
ting of bits,
as I clean
for the sound
in it,
a jet whine
home to New York
where long ago
a tall hoover
on carpets
old maroon
raised the wool
that sprung me.

GROGAN'S – SOUTH WILLIAM ST

The thumb is over
on my next finger
as I try to make
friends with myself

across gaps she filled
with her handbones, rings,
that held me together,
yet apart like a glove

separating ways of me
only now in touch
as I spend a pint of time
in the brown of Grogan's

a hedge of men along the wall
leaning down and back
and I hold my place,
say nothing of divorce

while on my lap
the rub and wrap
of skin tobacco gold,
the ten half-moons

twirl a feeling
I'm in with myself
and these hands
will not leave me alone.

BASEMENT – BY STEPHEN'S GREEN

The day is timed
by colour of light
come down to a flat
in the basement,
where I'm so still
I could be gone,
move only in skips
of the heart
and is it strong
enough to raise me
over the road,
to edge the circles
that meet under trees
beyond the benches
of men who wait
for the sun.

PLASTIC BAG – STEPHEN'S GREEN

I'm wandering over
tops of trees
in a winter park,
find on a limb
a plastic bag,
rustle it open
to hear compressed
a whisper of what
once I said
for better
or for worse,
and now I wonder
who keeps my words
in carrier bags,
lets them fly
and catch me
as they can,
even in the trees.

ST TERESA'S – CLARENDON STREET

The silence of St Teresa
as if she were alabaster
sent me out a side door
into the drench of an alley
four umbrellas wide
where I stood under awnings
by windows full of yellow
rings starry in the lights
and next to me a woman down
on cardboard begging shoppers
cutting in from Grafton Street
'Change Please, would you'
and it's only now I hear her.

TOUCHING MERCURY – KILDARE STREET

Double decker bus
beside me at the kerb
but I can't get on

for a space
as in a cinema
between the person
and the screen

keeps beyond me
what is near,
even though I taste

the breath
of passengers
as doors collapse.

Between eyes and mind
a feeling divides,
makes distant what I see

the Goodyear mark
on the big bus tyre
the winged foot
of Mercury

carries me away
until I touch his silver.

THE CAVE – STEPHEN'S GREEN

Haze of old gold
autumn sun
makes a shadowpark
and he is the boy
who after school
went to the zoo
in the Bronx
with a bag
of currant buns
to make friends
with the bears,

a huddle of them
waiting by the cave
for the buns to fly over
they'd catch in the air.

Today the same
scent of cold
in city centre air
as he lingers
under the scarlets
of a maple
in the Green,

a man thinking
of his winter
wishing it was as easy
as finding a cave
on the island
of rock and bramble
in the pond.

A SMALL CAFE – MONTAGUE STREET

At separate tables
pensioners having tea,
saucers over stains
on the tablecloths,
and I watch her head,
hair too black for it,
go down to a cup
steaming with the years,
follow the droops
of her coat, skirts,
see in a dark drape
shining white
the satin scallop
of her slip,
as if she had hidden
the last of her pride
like the promise
of a life still to come.

THE PLAYWRIGHT – HARCOURT STREET

I think George Fitzmaurice
you're not dead at all,
but still in that room
high up on the bricks,
and I'm not fooled
by the open air roof,
cementblock in the windows,
a bush growing in the chimney,
tricks I'd use myself.

I'm past your house
every morning for milk
knowing you're pages ahead
of me driven by the shiver
that comes with being alone,
having the words to yourself,
silent writer hearing the sound –
no wonder windows blocked
and all you need is sky.

SCRATCH CARDS – CUFFE STREET

A man not young
with no legs
wheels himself out
of a ground floor flat
on Cuffe Street,
shy at selling
what he holds
in his hands
for he'd know
what chance can bring,
but for the faith
he has in himself
buy his card,
pocket it on streets
where you'll never belong
and all that's left
are your legs.